職人という生き方

The Way of Life of Craftsmen

工匠的生活方式

江戸小紋

Edo Komon
江戸小紋

もくじ
Contents 目次

四代目 ── 廣瀬雄一さん 11
4th Generation
第四代
Yuichi Hirose
廣瀬雄一先生

江戸小紋の歴史 27
History of Edo Komon
江戸小紋的歷史

江戸小紋のつくり方 33
How to Produce Edo Komon
江戸小紋的製作方法

女性初 ── 岩下江美佳さん 39
The First Woman
首位女性
Emika Iwashita
岩下江美佳小姐

江戸小紋の道具 49
Tools and Equipments to Produce Edo Komon
江戸小紋的道具

江戸小紋の文様 59
Patterns of Edo Komon
江戸小紋的圖案

染付職人への道 65
Paths to Become a Dyeing Craftsman
成為染色工匠的路程

はじめに

Introduction 前言

　どうしたら職人になれるのか、といった問い合わせをよくいただくようになりました。ベテランの職人さんにうかがうと、技能を習得するためには柔軟性のある若いうちがよいとおっしゃいます。ワザの習得には10年近くの修行を必要としますから、若いうちに入門して20代半ばから後半で一人前になれれば、後の人生設計もたてやすいのでしょう。

　しかし、中学、高校を卒業後すぐに職人のもとに弟子入りするという道は、いまや険しいものです。弟子をとる余裕がないという職人の側の問題、若年層への職業教育の遅れ、高学歴化を進める画一的な進路指導などさまざまな要因が絡み合い、「若くして親方の元に弟子入り」という王道は姿を消しつつあります。

　インターネットサイト「ニッポンのワザドットコム」で取材を重ねる中で気づいたのは、いま職人への なり方はいくつもあるということです。畑違いの大学を出た後に家業を継ぐ。美大を卒業後、会社形態の工房に就職する。一度社会人になってから、自治体などの支援制度を利用して親方の元に弟子入りする。そのすべてに共通しているのは、情熱と根性が道を開くということです。好きであることが、何よりも大事な資質だとも言えます。

　職人になりたいと思ったら、ぜひ、どうしたらなれるのか自分で考えることをおすすめします。その際に、たくさんの先達の例を知ることは手助けになるはずです。伝統の世界に新しい風を運んでいるのが、ユニークな経歴をもつ職人や異業種から転身してきた職人である場合は少なくありません。厳しい環境を変えてゆく、新しい職人の健闘に心からエールを送りたいと思います。

6

We are frequently receiving inquiries from people asking in what way they can become craftsmen. In response to such questions, experienced craftsmen tell us that the best way would be to start learning techniques while young, that people have flexibility. As almost 10 years of training should be required to master such techniques, if they could start learning when young targeting to become a man by around middle or in the later half of twenties, it would reasonably allow them to design the rest of their life.

However, in reality today, to start being apprenticed with a craftsman right after graduating high or junior high school is not an easy way to take. Aspects such as economic difficulty for craftsmen to employ apprentices, backwardness of youth vocational education, and career guidance taken in an off-the-shelf manner at schools toward higher education, now twist together, resulting that the royal road "Start being apprenticed with craftsman while young" is at risk of being gone.

One thing we come across through interviews we conducted for our "nipponnowaza.com" website was that there are many different ways available for people who want to become craftsmen. For example, being the successor of his/her family business even after graduating a college of a different field, to start by finding job at a company-operated atelier after graduating art college, becoming an apprentice with a master by using publicly-offered supporting services of local governments even after being a member of society, for example. The common thing among all is that passion and guts open the door. That is to say, the most important qualification is that you love it.

Once you become interested in becoming craftsman, we therefore suggest you first to think, by your own, how you can make it real. While doing so, learning practices of your predecessors should be of help. Quite a lot of craftsmen, who breathe new sensitivity to the traditions, have unique background or have come from different fields. We would like to send hearty cheers to all such young craftsmen who strive to change today's tough environment for the better.

Editorial Department of "nipponnowaza.com"
October 2011
http://www.nipponnowaza.com

常有人問到，要怎樣才能夠成為工匠呢。經驗豐富的師傅認為，技能的學習要趁年輕柔軟性佳的時候。因為要學好一項技能，基本上需要將近10年的修行磨鍊，若能越早入門且在20歲前後就能獨當一面的話，之後的生涯規劃也會比較容易。

但是，在國中或是高中畢業後就立刻入門拜師學藝，現在說來是很沒保障的。工匠面臨的問題包括沒有空間可以收徒弟，對年輕一代的職業教育訓練太晚，還有在高學歷化的環境下，一成不變的前途規劃指導等各種原因錯綜複雜，「趁年輕時拜師學藝」這種理所當然的想法已經日漸式微。

由「日本的技藝.COM」網站多次的專訪中得知，現在要成為工匠有許多管道可以選擇。有人在大學畢業後選擇繼承和主修毫無相關的家業。像是美術大學畢業後，進入公司型態的工作室上班。先出社會上班一陣子，之後再利用自治團體等的補助制度選擇拜師學藝的道路。其共通點是，熱情和忍耐是成功的關鍵。「有興趣」，這點也可說是最重要的資質。

想當工匠的話，建議務必先試著自己想想如何才能達成。在這時候，前輩們的各種經驗談應該會是最佳的參考範例。擁有獨特經歷的工匠和從其他領域跨行而來的工匠也不在少數，他們為傳統世界帶來了新的風格。在此，對在艱險環境中努力奮鬥的工匠們，打從心裡給予最熱烈的掌聲。

2011年10月 日本的技藝.COM編輯部
http://www.nipponnowaza.com

四代目

4th Generation

第四代

廣瀬染工場・四代目 廣瀬雄一さん

The 4th generation at Hirose Senkoujou Yuichi Hirose

1918年（大正7年）創立の廣瀬染工場は、いまでも昔ながらの手染めにこだわり続けている数少ない染工場。お客さまとして尾上松緑、片岡仁左衛門など歌舞伎役者の名もあがる歴史ある染工場では、親子代々、そのこだわりとワザを継承してきました。

今回お話しをうかがった雄一さんは、廣瀬染工場の四代目。元ウィンドサーフィンオリンピック強化選手という、異色の経歴を持つ雄一さんですが、半纏を羽織ると一変、職人の顔になります。時代を感じさせる「板場」と呼ばれる工場で、仕事を拝見しながら、江戸小紋への思いをうかがいました。

プロフィール／有限会社廣瀬染工場・ひろせせんこうじょう 1918年（大正7年）創立の歴史ある江戸小紋の染工場。90年以上もの歳月、昔ながらの手染めにこだわって製作を続けている。1999年（平成11年）に三代目・廣瀬一成氏が国の伝統工芸士に認定。歌舞伎役者の着物を手がけるなど、そのワザに魅せられる人は多い。

Founded in 1918, Hirose Senkojo has hold its position as a dyeing factory dedicated in traditional hand dyeing. At the factory, time-honored with well-known Kabuki actors such as Shoroku Onoe and Nizaemon Kataoka, the formality and techniques have been upheld from generation to generation. Yuichi, whom we interviewed, is the 4th generation of Hirose Senkojo. Once he puts on his Hanten (a traditional working jacket), he, used to be named as a major candidate player of wind surfing for The Olympics one day, turns his face to that of craftsman. At the workplace called "Itaba" showing signs of is whole history, we interviewed him for his thought while observing his work.

1918年(大正7年)創立的廣瀬染工坊，是少數到現在仍然堅持傳統手染的染工坊。廣瀬染工坊擁有知名客戶，像是尾上松緑和片岡仁左衛門等知名的歌舞伎演員，堅持和技藝在此世世代代傳承著。這次拜訪的雄一先生，是廣瀬染工坊的第四代。據說雄一先生原先是奧運風浪板的重點培育選手，擁有這種特殊經歷的他，在披上工作服後，就會立即呈現出工匠的專注神情。他們將工坊稱為「板場」，在此可以感受到時代的變遷，亦能窺見雄一先生對江戸小紋的想法。

簡介／有限會社廣瀬染工坊・
EDO KOMON HIROSE dye-works
創立於1918年(大正7年)，是間擁有相當歷史的江戶小紋工坊，90多年以來堅持使用傳統手染製作。於1999年(平成11年)第三代的廣瀬一成先生榮獲認定為國家傳統工藝士。很多歌舞伎演員的戲服製作是在此製作完成的，其技藝之精巧讓人讚嘆不已。

Profile: Hirose Senkoujou Limited Company
A historical textile dyeing factory working on Edo Komon, founded in 1918. Over 90 years, the factory has kept is formality of traditional hand-dyeing techniques. The 3rd generation Kazunari Hirose was recognized by the nation as a Traditional Craftsman in 1999. A lot of people are fascinated with the techniques, as it supports some Kabuki actors for their Kimono.

廣瀬雄一さんは「廣瀬染工場」の四代目

Yuichi Hirose is the 4th generation of Hirose Senkojo.

廣瀬雄一先生是「廣瀬染工坊」的第四代

手染めの小紋染め。
伝統技術を継承する廣瀬染工場

　一見、無地のように見える絹の着物。しかし近くに寄って目をこらすと、極めて小さい模様の連続が浮かび上がり、そこに繊細な美が息づいているのが分かります。江戸小紋（東京染小紋）は、江戸時代の武士の礼装──裃（かみしも）の柄から発展したもので、単色で染めた細かい紋様が特徴。1952年に文化財保護委員会（現在の文化庁）が、当時小紋染めの名人として活躍していた小宮康助氏の技術を認め、重要無形文化財として選定。ほかの小紋染めと区別するために「江戸小紋」と命名し誕生しました。

　今回訪問した「廣瀬染工場」は、大正7年（1918年）に創立。90年以上にも渡り、伝統文化を受け継いできた歴史ある工場です。お話をうかがったのは、元ウインドサーフィンオリンピック強化選手という経歴を持つ、廣瀬染工場の四代目　廣瀬雄一さん。父親は、歌舞伎役者・尾上松緑、片岡仁左衛門らの着物を染めるなど、多方面で活躍する伝統工芸士・廣瀬一成（かずなり）さん。廣瀬染工場は、近年、機械染に移行する工場が多い中、今でも昔ながらの手付け（手染め）

型彫と型付け、染めの一体技術で
つくりあげる多彩な表情

にこだわり続けています。板場と呼ばれる工場にはひんやりとした空気が漂い、染料のにおいが立ちこめていました。白生地が張られた長さ7メートルもあるモミの木の張板の脇に立ち、防染糊を伸ばしながら型付けをする雄一さん。天井を見上げると、何十年も使い込まれた風合いの張板が何枚も吊られていました。この場所で、室町時代にまで遡るという東京染小紋のワザが今なお受け継がれているのです。

「よい型彫師がいなければ、江戸小紋は滅びる」と言われるほど、江戸小紋と伊勢型紙の関係性は緊密。江戸小紋をはじめ、型友禅などの染色工程で用いられる伊勢型紙は、柿渋を塗り張り合わせた美濃紙を用いてつくられます。三重県鈴鹿市の白子を主な生産地とし、職人が専用の彫刻刀で——極小の宇宙とも呼ばれる——精緻な文様を彫りぬきます。

At the stenciling "Katatsuke" process, they repeat putting a silk fabric on a single board, putting a template, and placing resist paste.

「印模」時將絲綢底布蓋在木板上，印模後施加防染糊，如此不斷重覆操作。

「型付け」では一枚板に絹地を張りつけ、型を当て防染糊を置くことを繰り返します。

大正7年に創業した「廣瀬染工場」。板場の天井には何枚もの張板が吊られています

Hirose Senkojo, founded in 1918. Number of boards called "Hariita" are hung from the ceiling.

創立於大正7年的「廣瀬染工坊」。板場的天花板上吊掛著幾片張板。

四代目、廣瀬雄一さんと、
この道50年という職人の森谷さん

The 4th generation Yuichi Hirose, and Mr. Moriya who has served as a craftsman for 50 years.

第四代的廣瀬雄一先生與有50年資歷的森谷先生。

廣瀬染工場の「型紙部屋」を見せてもらいました。裸電球がぶら下がる四畳半ほどの部屋に、所狭しと積まれる古い型紙。「ここにあるものだけで、新旧併せ4000種類を超えると思います。中には人間国宝の方が彫られた型紙もあるんですよ」と雄一さん。江戸小紋の神髄ともいえる文様の美が凝縮された型紙は、代々大切に受け継いでいくそう。

さて、型付けを終えた雄一さんは、染料を溶かした色糊を生地に引く「シゴキ」作業に入りました。「シゴキの前に色合わせをして、不純物を取り除き、糊をよりきめ細かくするために、サラシでこします」。柄のついた白生地に色糊を引き、その後上からオガクズを均一にかけます。これは、生地を折り畳んで蒸し箱に入れたとき、糊と糊が付かないようにするため。90度の蒸し箱で約30分間蒸され、色を定着させた生地は次に水槽で水洗い。天日で乾燥させて完成です。「色の具合は、天候や湿度によって都度変わります。染め上がりが楽しみなのと同時に心配にもなりますね」。

そんな多くの工程を経て、江戸小紋は完成。古くより変わらぬ日々の技術を地道に繰り返しながら、伝統は継承されています。

連絡先／有限会社廣瀬染工場　住所／東京都新宿区中落合 4-32-5
電話／ 03-3951-2155
HP ／ http://komonhirose.co.jp/

Contact information: Hirose Senkojo Limited Company, Address: 4-32-5 Nakaochiai, Shinjuku-ku, Tokyo
Telephone: 03-3951-2155
Website: http://komonhirose.co.jp/

聯絡處／有限會社廣瀬染工坊　地址／東京都新宿区中落合4-32-5
電話／03-3951-2155
網址／http://komonhirose.co.jp/

廣瀬染工場の「型紙部屋」には、新旧併せ4000種類を超える型紙が保管されています
In the template storage room of Hirose Senkojo, more than 4,000 different templates, old and new, are stored.
在廣瀬染工坊的「模紙室」裡珍藏著4000種以上的新舊模紙。

小紋や友禅などの着物の染色に
古くから用いられてきた伊勢型紙。
型紙の中に精緻な美が凝縮されています

Ise templates, traditionally used for dyeing of Kimono such as Komon and Yuzen. Elements of sophisticated beauty of Kimono are packed together in these templates.

伊勢模紙自古廣泛用於小紋與友禪的布料染色。模紙中凝聚了無以倫比的精緻之美。

3 1
4 2

3. 蒸し箱で約30分間。染料を定着させます
4. 水洗いし、糊や余分な染料を落とします

3. Put it into a steaming chamber for about 30 minutes to make dye permanently set.
4. Wash away paste and extra dye with water.

3. 置於蒸箱約半小時。如此可以使染料滲透
4. 用水清洗可除去多餘的色糊與染料

1. 染料を溶かした色糊を塗る「シゴキ」
2. 色糊を引き終えたら、オガクズをまぶします

1. "Shigoki" process, placing color starch made with melted dye.
2. After placing color starch, sprinkle with sawdust.

1.「染底色」作業，塗上含有染料的色糊
2. 完成塗色糊的作業後，接著灑上碎木屑

Hirose Senkojo challenges in new fields as well. They reflect Edo's style into interior products and daily items by using their Some-Komon techniques.

廣瀨染工坊也試著挑戰新領域。染小紋的技術也運用在室內飾品與日常用品，將江戶經典融入生活之中。

廣瀨染工場では新しい分野へも挑戦。インテリア、日常の小物にも染小紋の技術を用い江戸の粋を映し込みます

Komonzome by hand dyeing.

Hirose Senkojo, upholding the traditional techniques.

A silk Kimono, that looks unpatterned at a glance. But taking a closer look, you will find extremely detailed patterns progressibely located and delicate beauty is engrained there. Edo Komon (Tokyo Some-Komon) has developed out of patterns of a formal dress called Kamishimo featured with fine patterns dyed in single color for Samurai in Edo Period. In 1952, Cultural Properties Protection Committee (Agency for Cultural Affairs today) recognized Kosuke Komiya for his Komon-zome expertise and appointed him an Important Intangible Cultural Heritage. The technique was then named Edo Komon to distinguish from the other types of Komon-zome.

Hirose Senkojo we visited was founded in 1918. It is a factory consistently held up its traditional culture for more than 90 years. The person we interviewed was Yuichi Hirose, the 4th generation of Hirose Senkojo and has a background of being appointed as a major candidate player of wind surfing for The Olympics. His father Kazunari Hirose, named as a Traditional Craftsman, who actively works in a variety of field such as dyeing Kimono for Kabuki actors Shoroku Onoe and Nizaemon Kataoka. Hirose Senkojo still maintains its position of staying with traditional hand dyeing (Tetsuke) while more and more factories go for machined dyeing. In the workplace called Itaba, cool air was floating and filled with smell of dye. Standing next to a Hariita in length of 7 meters made of fir tree covered with a white cloth, Yuichi puts resist paste and performs stenciling (Katatsuke). Looking up the ceiling, we found a lot of Hariita hung, that looked being used throughout decades. Techniques to produce Tokyo Komon-zone, date back to Muromachi Period, is certainly upheld even today.

Template making, stenciling, and dyeing.

A consecutive work realizes prismatic aspect.

As it is said "Without having skilled template engraver, Edo Komon will become destroyed", Edo Komon and Ise templates are closely linked together. Ise templates, used not only for Edo Komon but also for dyeing process of Kata Yuzen for example, are made with layered Mino paper with sour persimmon paste put in between. Shiroko of Suzuka City, Mie Prefecture is a major place of the manufacturing, and craftsmen work out the sophisticated patterns – called a micro space – by using carving knives designed for it.

We were allowed to step in their template storage room. In the floor space of around 4.5 tatami mats, under naked light bulbs, we found old tempates stacked up closely together. "I think we have more than 4,000 different old and new templates, at least right here. It is not too much to say this place is the heart of us. Some of these were done by Living National Treasures indeed." Yuichi explains. These templates, in that the beauty of patterns are packed together and are recognized as the soul of Edo Komon, will be handed over generation after generation.

Well, upon stenciling finished, Yuichi started to perform "Shigoki" process that s color starch made with melted dye is put on a white cloth. "Before doing Shigoki, I perform color matching, remove impurities, and get the color starch strained through a bleached cotton cloth in order to make it finer.". On a white cloth with handles, he puts color starch, then sprinkle sawdust on top evenly. This process is in order not to make the folded cloth stuck together by color starch when put into a steaming chamber. Having steamed at 90 degrees C for about 30 minutes in a chamber, the color is permanently set and the cloth is washed in a water tank. The whole process ends with drying in the sun. "Texture of color appears differently upon weather and humidity. Always I can't wait for finish of dyeing but I am always anxious also.". Going through such a variety of processes, Edo Komon becomes finished. By tracing techniques unchanged from old days on a consistent manner, tradition is handed over to the next generations.

手染的小紋染。繼承傳統技藝的廣瀨染工坊

乍看之下絲綢和服像是素色的。不過當走近凝神注視時，就會浮現出連續不斷的細紋，其呈現出的是纖細且生動的美感。江戶小紋（東京染小紋）是從江戶時代的武士禮服──裃的花紋發展而來的，其特徵是單色渲染的纖細花紋。1952年，當時小宮康助先生以小紋染名家的身分聞名於世，其技藝受到文化財保護委員會（現在的文化廳）的認同，同時獲選認定為重要無形文化財。為了有別於其他的小紋染，「江戶小紋」從此得名誕生。

這次採訪的「廣瀨染工坊」創立於大正7年（1918年）。擁有90年以上的歷史，不斷延續著傳統文化的傳承。接受採訪的是廣瀨雄一先生。他曾經是奧運風浪板的重點培育選手，現在是廣瀨染工坊的第四代。他父親廣瀨一成先生曾獲選為傳統工藝士，在許多方面都相當傑出，也曾為歌舞伎演員尾上松綠和片岡仁左衛門等人手染製作過戲服。近年來許多工坊都轉為機械染製，但廣瀨染工坊現在仍堅持繼續傳統的手工染製（手染）。他們稱工坊為板場，這裡的涼爽空氣裡夾帶著染料的味道。雄一先生站在鋪有全白紡織品，長達7公尺的樅木板旁，塗抹防染糊同時決定花紋。抬頭仰望天花板，那裡吊掛著好多片看起來已經使用數十年的木板。在這裡，至今仍傳承著源自於室町時代的東京染小紋技藝。

用雕模、印模與染色的整體技術來營造出豐富多彩的風格

「若沒有優秀的雕模師，江戶小紋就會絕跡」，如同這樣的說法，江戶小紋與伊勢模紙的關係密不可分。用於江戶小紋、型友禪等染色作業的伊勢模紙，是用塗上柿澀黏貼而成的美濃紙來製作的。三重縣鈴鹿市白子是其主要產地，工匠專用的雕刻刀──也被稱為極小宇宙──能夠雕刻出纖細的圖案。

我們探訪了廣瀨染工坊的「模紙室」。那是一處約四疊半（約二坪）面積的小房間，上頭懸掛舊式燈泡，四處堆滿著舊模紙。

雄一先生說道：「我想這裡的新舊模紙加起來應該超過4000種。說這裡是我們工坊的心臟也不為過。裡面也有國寶級人物所雕製作的模紙呢。」模紙上鏤刻著的絢爛圖案，那可說是江戶小紋的精華所在，看樣子要代代傳承應該不是問題。

雄一先生完成印模後，接著開始進行「染底色」作業，亦即將摻有染料的色糊抹平。「染底色」前須先對色、去除雜質，並用濾布過篩，可使色糊更顯細緻。將色糊塗抹在帶有花飾的白底上，再均勻灑下碎的木屑。這道製程是為了使布折疊堆放入蒸箱時，避免色糊互相黏著在一起。置入90度的蒸箱內熱蒸約半小時，接著將完成染色的布放入水槽內清洗，再以陽光使之乾燥後即完工。「顏色會因天氣或濕度的不同而有所變化。期待完工的同時也一邊擔心著顏色問題呢。」

經過繁瑣的多道製程，江戶小紋即大功告成。亙古不變的傳統技藝，現在仍在此反覆且紮實地持續傳承中。

廣瀨染工場・作品
Works of Hirose Senkojo
廣瀨染工坊的作品

江戸小紋の歴史

History of Edo Komon

江戸小紋的歷史

矢場女艶姿立図 蹄斎北馬
江戸時代文化頃（1804年頃）

Yaba-Onna Adesugata Tachizu Hokuba Teisai
Bunka, Edo Period (in around 1804)

揶聲女艶姿立圖 蹄齋北馬 江戸時代文化時期

An autograph Ukiyoe drawn by Hokuba Teisai, an apprentice of Hokusai Katsushika. The woman drawn is a Yatorime. In Edo, there were amusement areas called Yaba where people could enjoy shooting arrows, and it is said their business went well as beautiful Yatorime (women who pick up and collect arrows) they hired successfully attracted male guests. The Komon is drawn quite in detail, a Tenugui (towel) to keep her hair free from dust, and the bamboo leaves drawn on Kimono and the Obi implying that the client might have some relation with bamboo leaves. Through the combination of textures and color matching observed, you can learn of the mode of life in that Period.

葛飾北斎の弟子である蹄斎北馬によって描かれた、肉筆の浮世絵。描かれている女性は、矢取り女。江戸では、矢場という楊弓を射させる娯楽場があり、美女の矢取り女を雇って、それを目当てにお客を呼び繁盛させたといいます。大変丁寧に描かれた小紋が素晴らしく、髪に巻いた埃よけの手拭い、またこの図の依頼主が笹に関係があるのか、着物と帯には笹が描かれています。柄合わせや色使いなど、この時代の風俗を楽しむことができます。

此畫為葛飾北齋的門徒、蹄齋北馬親筆所繪之浮世繪。畫中的女性為拾箭女。當時江戶城內設有小型弓箭的射箭遊樂場，他們雇用貌美的年輕女子負責拾箭，藉以攬客使之生意興隆。畫上描繪著令人讚嘆的纖細小紋，女性將手帕置於頭髮上防止灰塵，另外，這幅畫的委託人不知是否與竹子有所淵源，和服及腰帶上都繪有竹子圖案。可從花樣及上色欣賞這個時代的風俗情趣。

協力／羽黒洞　住所／東京都文京区湯島 4-6-11　湯島ハイタウン
電話／03-3815-0431　営業時間／ 11:00 〜 6:30　定休日／日曜休廊
HP ／ http://www.hagurodo.jp

Courtesy / Hagurodo, Address: Yushima Hightown, 4-6-11 Yushima, Bunkyo-ku, Tokyo
Telephone: 03-3805-0431, Opening hours: 11:00 – 18:30, Closed: Sundays
Website: http://www.hagurodo.jp

協贊／羽黑洞　地址／東京都文京區湯島4-6-11 湯島 High Town
電話／03-3815-0431　營業時間／ 11:00 〜 18:30　公休日／週日
網址／ http://www.hagurodo.jp

室町時代の武家から発祥。武士や町人に広がり、江戸の粋に

　室町時代に、武家が所有する鎧の革所（かわどころ／皮革で作られた部分）や家紋に使われたのが、江戸小紋の始まりだといわれています。江戸時代に入ると、全国から江戸（東京）に集まる大名とともに武士が増加。そのため、武士の裃（かみしも／礼装のひとつ）小紋が生産されるようになりました。

　江戸時代中期には、町人の着物に小紋が施され、江戸の粋な着物として普及。江戸の人々に愛されるようになったのです。明治時代以降は、訪問着など女性の着物として発展しています。

Originated from samurai families in Muromachi Period.
Spread to samurais and common citizens, then became Edo's style.
It is said that symbols put on Kawadokoro (parts made with leather) of Yoroi and used as crests of Samurai families in Muromachi Period are the origins of Edo Komon. Later in Edo Period, number of samurais coming up to Edo (Tokyo) accompanying feudal lords started increasing. Consequently, Kamishimo (one of formal dresses of samurai) Komon started being produced. In the middle of Edo Period, Komon stareted being put also on Kimono of common citizens, and became popular as Edo's style. People in Edo well accepted the style. In Meiji Period and later, the Kimono developed to women's one such as ceremonial dress.

發揚於室町時代的武士之家
盛行於武士及商人之間並成為江戶的經典
在室町時代，據傳江戶小紋的開始是武士將其用於盔甲的皮革處(用皮革製作的部分)或是家徽上。進入江戶時代後，江戶城(東京)內增加了許多來自全國各地的諸侯與武士，因此有工匠開始製作武士的小紋禮服。到了江戶中期，商人們的和服上也出現了小紋圖案，因而小紋成了江戶的經典服飾且開始普及，廣受江戶人們喜愛。明治時代以後，逐漸演變為女性所穿的正式禮服。

江戸小紋のつくり方

How to Produce Edo Komon

江戸小紋的製作方法

少しのズレで台無しに。
彫師と染付職人が織り成すワザ

　江戸小紋は、型紙をつくる彫師と、染める染付職人の共同作業で完成します。型紙は主に、伊勢型紙を使用。染付職人は、彫師が彫刻刀でつくりだした細かい模様の型紙を受け継ぐことから始まります。

　まず、色糊（いろのり／染料を混ぜた糊）を調整。染め上がりを左右する色糊には、職人の熟練したワザが要求されます。次に、生地に型紙をのせて、防染糊（ぼうせんのり）を置く型付け。細かな模様のため、髪の毛一本でもずれると、生地に線が入ってしまう極めて難しい作業です。その後、板干し、地色染め、蒸し、水洗いを経て、乾燥仕上げで完成です。

Misalignment, even slight, makes all ruined.
Techniques collaboratively brought by template engraver and dyeing craftsman.
Edo Komon is completed through coorperative work by engraver who makes template paper and dyeing craftsman who performs dyeing. Template paper is primarily made with Ise template paper. Dyeing craftsman starts working by receiving template with detailed patterns engraver created by using carving knives. First, dyeing craftsman makes necessary adjustments of color starch. The process, affecting quality of dyeing, requires highly skilled craftsman's techniques. Next is stenciling, placing template on the white cloth, then putting resist paste. This is a technically difficult process because the pattern is detailed and, misalignment, even for diameter of single hair, gives the white cloth undesired lines. Going through Itaboshi, base-color dyeing, steaming, water wash, and drying, Edo Komon becomes complete.

稍有偏差就會前功盡棄。
融合雕模師與染色工匠的技藝
江戶小紋須由製作模紙的雕模師與染色工匠共同作業才能完成。模紙主要採用伊勢模紙。雕模師以雕刻刀纖細刻割模紙之後，接下來便交由染色工匠進行作業。首先，要調整色糊（摻入顏料的漿糊），由於色糊會影響染色後的質感，因此工匠們必須具備非常熟練的染色技巧。接著，將模紙放在底布上，並塗上防染糊進行印模。江戶小紋非常精緻，染色過程中，即便只是沾上一根毛髮都會破壞圖樣，過程相當困難。之後還要經過木板烘乾、附模入底、熱蒸、水洗、乾燥等多道製程才算完成。

型紙の彫刻
雕刻模紙
Template making by engraving

色糊の調整
調整色糊
Adjustment of color starch

型付け
印模
Katatsuke

板干し
以木板烘乾
Itaboshi (Drying on a board)

乾燥仕上げ	水洗い	蒸し	地色染め
乾燥完成	水洗	熱蒸	附模入底
Drying for finish	Washing with water	Steaming	Base color dyeing

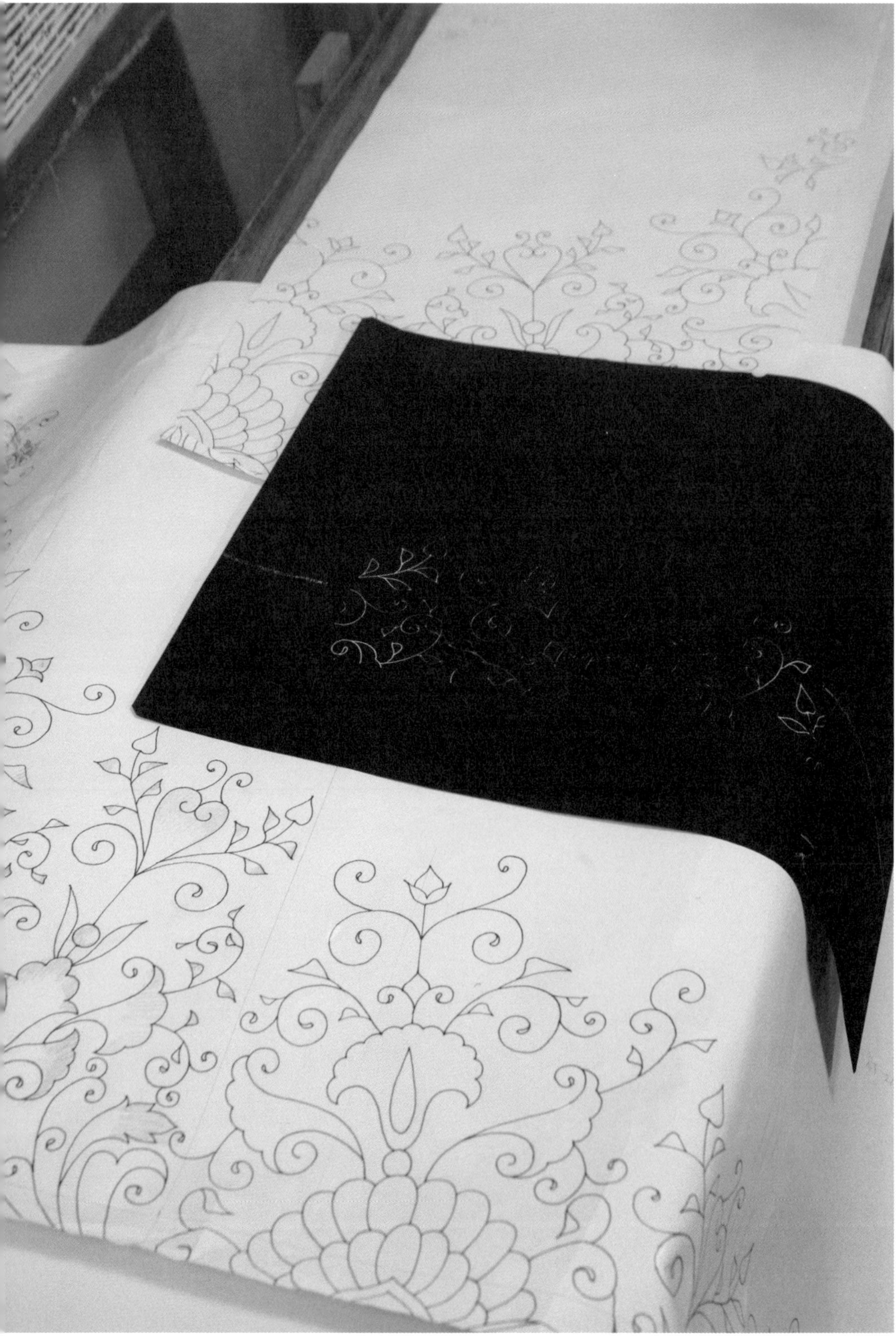

女性初

The First Woman

首位女性

岩下江美佳さん

Emika Iwashita
岩下江美佳小姐

伝統工芸の世界に清新な風を送り込む一人の女性。
女性で初めて江戸小紋(東京染小紋)の伝統工芸士に認定されたのが岩下江美佳さんです。
女性らしい柔らかなデザインは、岩下さんの雰囲気そのもの。
しかし相当の覚悟と根性がなくては、こうして一人前の職人として独立することは出来なかったに違いありません。
マンションの一室に「手づくりした」という工房(板場)で、お話をうかがってきました。

A woman, who breathes new sensitivity to the world of traditional art. The first woman recognized as a Traditional Craftsman of Edo Komon (Tokyo Some-Komon) is Emika Iwashita. The gentle and feminine design, represents her mood itself. However, it is easy to imagine that she would never become an independent craftsman unless committing herself heavily and having guts. We visited her for interview at her atelier (Itaba) that she "set up by herself" inside an apartment.

這位女性為傳統工藝的世界帶來了一股清新徹風。她就是首位獲得江戶小紋(東京染小紋)傳統工藝士認證的女性──岩下江美佳小姐。女性特有的溫柔,即是岩下小姐獨特的設計風格。但是,若沒有相當的醒悟與天份,絕對是無法成為獨當一面的工匠。讓我們前往這間位於大樓裡,名為「手工製作」的工作室(板場),探訪這名首位女性染色工匠。

プロフィール/岩下江美佳・いわしたえみか 1973年東京生まれ。武蔵野美術大学短期大学部工芸デザイン テキスタイルコース卒業後、株式会社富田染工芸入社。2007年、女性で初の東京染小紋伝統工芸士に認定。2008年独立。『粋凜香(すいりんか)』は自身のブランド。

簡介/岩下江美佳(Emika IWASHITA)1973年生於東京,畢業於武藏野美術大學短期大學部工藝設計系紡織類群。畢業後就進入富田染工藝股份有限公司工作。2007年獲選為首位東京染小紋傳統工藝士認證的女性。2008年自立門戶,創立個人品牌『粋凜香』。(雅號為岩下櫻佳)

Profile: Emika Iwashita, born in Tokyo, 1973. After graduating Art Design & Textile course of Musashino Junior College of Art and Design, joined Tomita Senkogei Co., Ltd.. In 2007, she became the first woman recognized as a Traditional Craftsman of Tokyo Some-Komon. Became independent in 2008. "Sui Rin Ka" is her own brand.

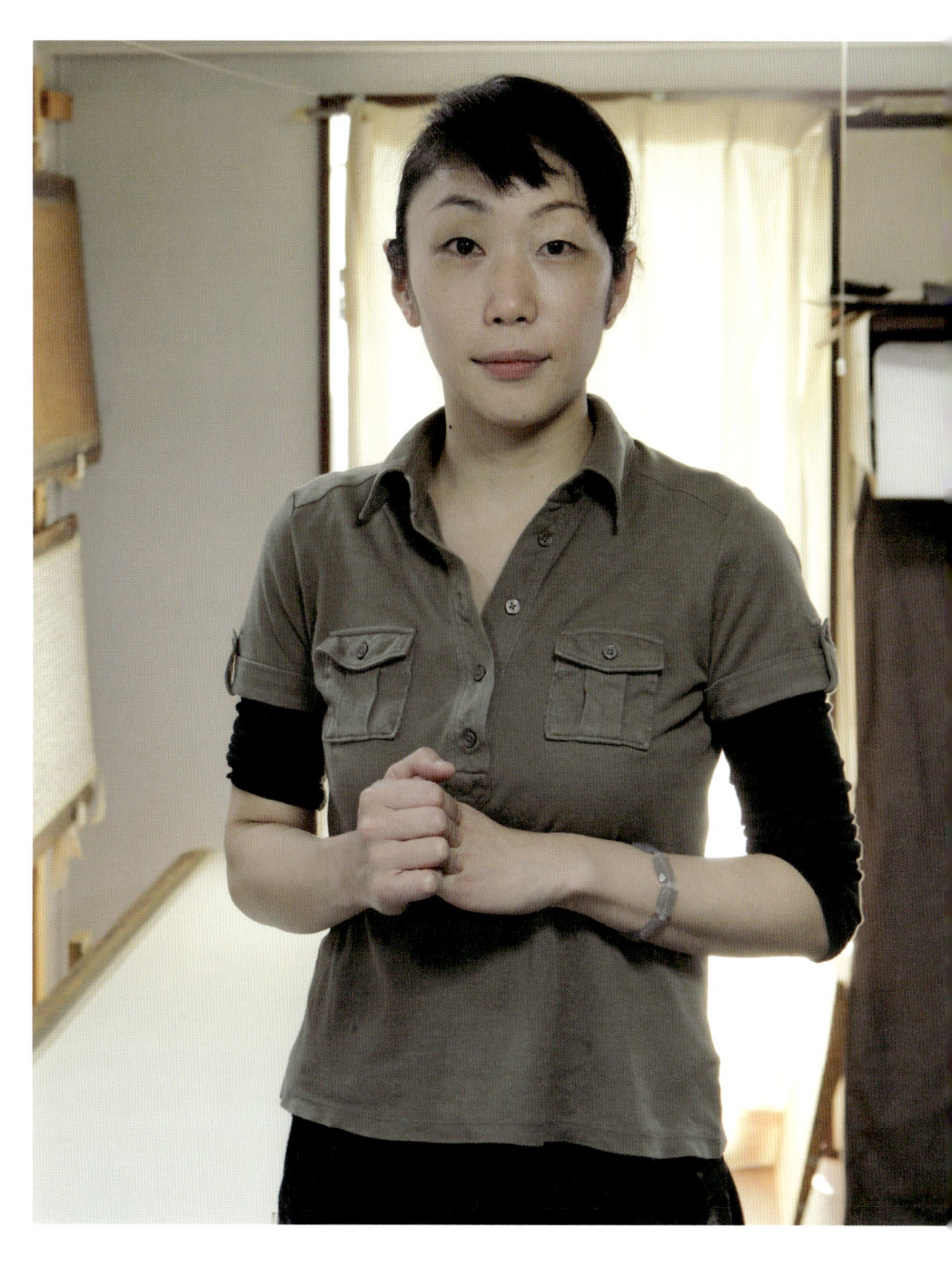

岩下江美佳さんは、2007年に、江戸小紋（東京染小紋）で女性では初めてという伝統工芸士に認定されました

Emika Iwashita became the first woman recognized as Traditional Craftsman of Edo Komon (Tokyo Some-Komon) in 2007.

岩下江美佳小姐，於2007年成為首位榮獲江戶小紋（東京染小紋）傳統工藝士認證的女性。

女性初の伝統工芸士
岩下江美佳さん

古い町工場の建ち並ぶ、下町のマンションの一室にそのアトリエはありました。部屋の間仕切りをすべて取り払い、長さ約7メートルの一枚板を横たえて黙々と作業をする女性。2007年に、江戸小紋で女性では初めてという伝統工芸士に認定された岩下江美佳さんです。

「親戚が呉服店をしているため、幼い頃から着物に親しんでいました」と話す岩下さん。江戸小紋に魅せられ、美術大学のテキスタイル科を卒業後、親族の反対を押し切って新宿区の染工房で働いたのち独立。現在『粋凛香（すいりんか）』という自らのブランドを持ち、多くの作品を発表しています。

「この板場は全部手づくりなんです。ホームセンターで照明を揃えて、クレーンを使って窓から40キロの板を運び入れて。本当に大変でした（笑）」。

着物が大好きな女の子だったという岩下さん。呉服店を継いだ叔

父の「着物は身にまとう絵画だ」という言葉に感銘を受け、自分でもそんな素敵なものをつくりたいと思うようになったと言います。

型紙に印された柄と柄を丁寧に重ねる「合わせ星」を確認しながら、使い込みすり減ったヘラを巧みに動かし生地に文様を写していく岩下さん。腰を落とし、何度も同じことを繰り返す作業で、体を壊したこともあったそうですが、伝統工芸の道を諦めることはありませんでした。

「江戸小紋はこれまで男の世界でした。だから、女性ならではの目線でおしゃれで、気軽に着られるようなものを提案していきたいですね」。

時代は変わり、後継者不足を叫ばれる江戸小紋。しかし時を超えてその美しさに魅せられた人たちが、都市のなかで静かに、脈々と技を受け継いでいるのです。

40キロもあるという長い張板を運び、都内のマンションの一室を板場として作業している岩下さん。
板場を閉め切り、温度と湿度に気をつけて型付けを行います

Iwashita works on a long Hariita board weighing as heavy as 40kg that she brought in a room of an apartment located in Tokyo that she uses as her atelier. With all the doors and windows closed, she performs stenciling with attention to temperature and humidity.

岩下小姐自己想辦法將重達40公斤的張板搬進大樓裡，接著就把這裡當成了板場開始作業。
板場內須密閉，且要注意溫度與濕度以進行印模作業。

ムラが出ないように、
水平にゆっくりとヘラを走らせます

She sweeps a paddle horizontally on a gentle manner
not to make it uneven.

握住刮刀小心地水平移動，以保持刮面的均一平整

型紙についた星を合わせ、
慎重に文様をつなぎます

Correctly locate star marks of template,
and carefully align the patterns with others.

對齊模紙上的記號，小心慎重地蓋上圖案

使い込み、すり減ったヒノキのヘラ。
新品と比べてみれば分かります

Worn paddles made with cypress tree.
Comparable with new one.

久用磨耗後的檜木材質刮刀。新舊兩者的差異一目瞭然

水につけてよく伸ばした型紙に
防染糊を置き型付けを行います

Perform stenciling by putting resist paste on a template
that is well stretched by being put into water.

沾水以使模紙更加伸展，接著塗上防染糊進行印模作業。

The first woman of Traditional Craftsman Emika Iwashita

In an apartment based in a downtown of Tokyo where number of old small factories stand side by side, we found her atelier. Having all the partitions removed away, a woman silently works on a board in length as long as 7 meters put on the floor. She is Emika Iwashita, the first woman recognized as a Traditional Craftsman in 2007.

"I have already been familialized with Kimono since childhood because my relatives were running a Kimono shop.", Iwashita explains. Being fascinated with Edo Komon and graduating a textile course of an art college, and after working for a certain period at a dyeing factory based in Shinjuku, Tokyo despite opposition from her family, she became an independent craftsman. Now she has her own brand "Sui Rin Ka" and releases a lot of works.

"All here at this Itaba (workplace) are what I have done by myself. Lightings were purchased at a do-it-yourself store, and I used a crane to bring a board weighing 40kg into here. All were tough work though :)."

Iwashita, who says used be a girl really loved Kimono. She explains that she became aspired to being a producer of such beautiful things because of being impressed with her uncle's words "Kimono is a painting for people to put on.".

Iwashita performs transferring patterns of tempate to white cloth by carefully sweeping a worn paddle, while keeping the patterns of template aligned with the corresponding star marks. Although she had got sick from repeating the process in a kneeling position, she had never given up her career in traditional art.

"Edo Komon has long been positioned a world of men. So my idea is, from a women's viewpoint, to keep offering something more fashionable and being more casually acceptable.".

Time changes, and lack of successors is coming up as an issue around Edo Komon field. Despite the fact, there are such people who are fascinated with the beauty transcended the time, uphold the techniques silently and consistently even in a big city.

首位女性傳統工藝士岩下江美佳小姐

在舊式小工廠林立的老街上，有一間位於公寓內的工作室。房間的隔牆已全部拆除，在一塊長約7公尺的木板上，有位默默工作的女性。她就是2007年在江戶小紋業界第一位被認定為傳統工藝士的女性，岩下江美佳小姐。

岩下小姐說：「由於有親戚在經營和服店，因而從小就常接觸和服」。受到江戶小紋的魅力所吸引，從美術大學的服裝科畢業後，不顧家人反對在新宿區的染工房工作，之後獨自創業。現在擁有名為『粹凜香』的自創品牌，並且也發表了許多作品。

「這間工作室全部都是我自己親手做的。先去家用品量販店採買照明設備，接著用起重機從窗戶吊進40公斤重的木板。真是很辛苦啊(笑)」。

岩下小姐說自己曾經非常喜歡和服。繼承和服店的叔父曾說：「和服是穿在身上的繪畫」，受到這句話的感動，自己也想創作那樣美麗的東西。

岩下小姐一邊確認模紙上層層花樣的「對齊記號」，一邊細心地移動一支已用到磨損的刮刀，小心翼翼地在布料上描繪圖案。只要一坐下來就會開始重複好幾次相同的工作，聽說她也曾經差一點搞壞身子，但從沒想過要放棄傳統工藝這條路。

岩下小姐說：「江戶小紋一直都是男人的世界。因此，我想以女性的觀點，製作出具有時尚感，又可以輕鬆穿著的衣物」。

隨著時代的變遷，江戶小紋業界一直處於後繼無人的狀態。但是超越時空，江戶小紋的美仍讓許多人沈醉不已，他們正在都市的一角，脈脈地傳承著這項技藝。

お問合わせ／（株）江紋屋　住所／東京都中央区日本橋人形町 3-6-3 人形町イースト 208
電話／ 03-6206-2977

Contact information: Emon-ya Corporation
Address: 208, Ningyocho East, 3-6-3 Nihonbashi-Ningyocho, Chuo-ku, Tokyo
Telephone: 03-6206-2977

聯絡處／株式會社江紋屋
地址／東京都中央區日本橋人形町3-6-3人形町East 208
電話　03-6206-2977

端切れをスクラップした「作品集」を見せてもらいました

She showed us her "portfolio", a scrap of pieces of cloths she has worked out.

貼有多年創作樣本的「作品集」。

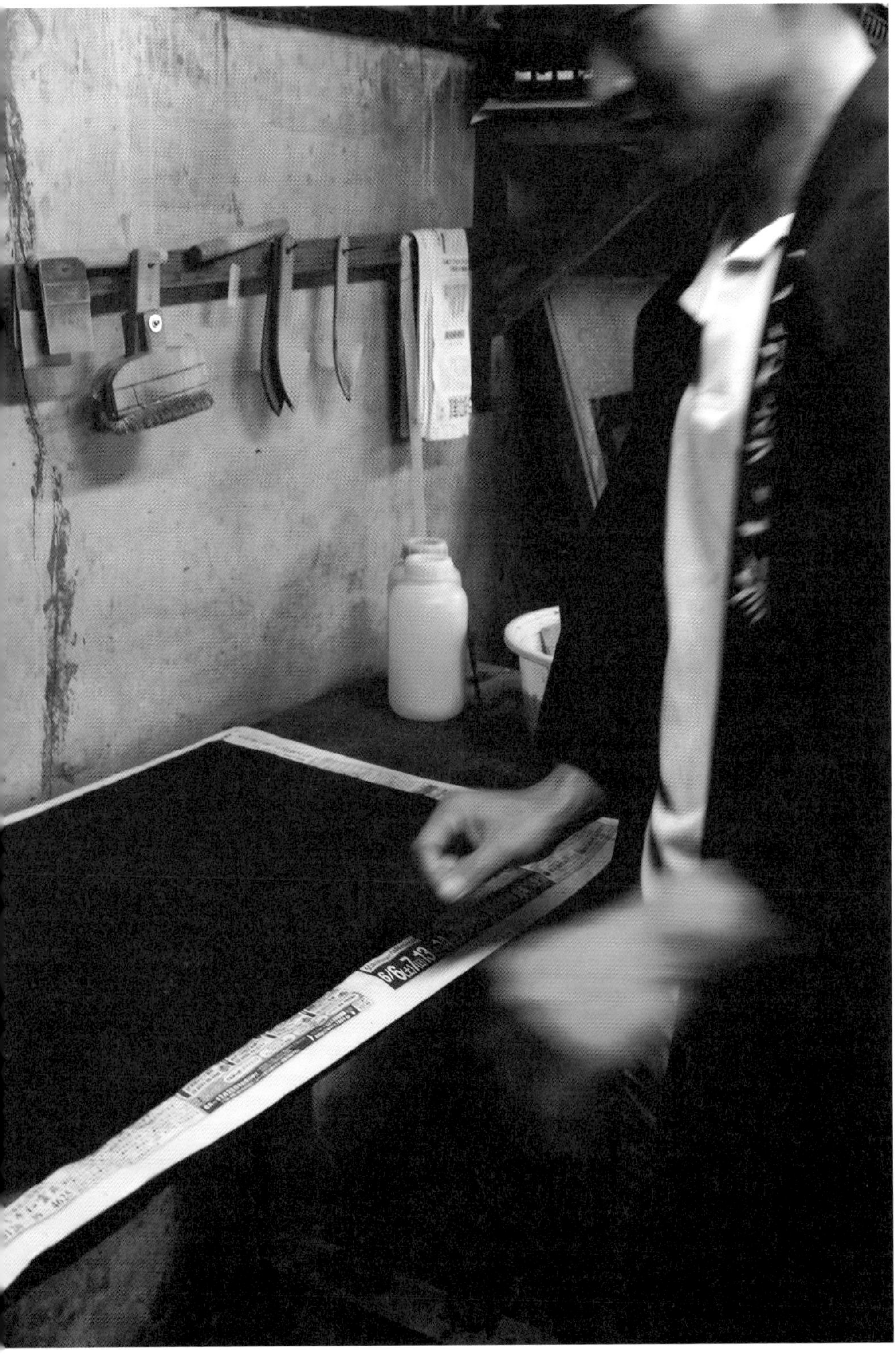

江戸小紋の道具

Tools and Equipments to Produce Edo Komon

江戸小紋的道具

職人のワザと文様の美が凝縮。人の手の温もり伝える伊勢型紙

染小紋で用いられる道具は数多くありますが、なかでも同じ伝統的工芸品である伊勢型紙は、とても関係性が深いものです。三重県鈴鹿市の白子を主な生産地とする伊勢型紙は、柿渋を塗り張り合わせた美濃紙に、職人が専用の彫刻刀で細かい文様を彫り抜いてつくられます。江戸小紋を始め、型友禅、浴衣などの染色工程で用いられ、その精緻な模様は極小の宇宙とも呼ばれるほど。突彫（つきぼり）、錐彫（きりぼり）、道具彫（どうぐぼり）、縞彫（しまぼり）、それに付属する技法として、縞柄などの型を補強する糸入れと呼ばれる五つの彫刻技法があり、それらはすべて機械では出せない緻密さと人の手の温もりを備えています。近年は染色用具に留まらず、襖や欄間、雪見障子、屏風などのインテリアや美術工芸品としても注目を集めています。

凝縮了工匠絕技和紋飾之美。
傳遞著手工質感的伊勢模紙
用於染小紋的道具很多，其中伊勢模紙也同樣是傳統工藝品，兩者有相當深厚的淵源。伊勢模紙主要生產於三重縣鈴鹿市的白子，工匠在塗抹了柿澀的美濃紙上，以專用的雕刻刀雕琢出細緻的文樣圖案製作而成。用於江戶小紋、型友禪、浴衣等染色作業，其精緻的模樣幾乎能稱之為微型宇宙。突雕、錐雕、道具雕、縞雕，還有其附屬技法，也就是用來補強縞雕花樣的入線，用這五種技巧可以達成機械無法做到的纖細和手工的質感。近年不只染色用具，在拉門、格窗、賞雪障門、屏風等室內裝飾品和美術工藝品方面也同樣受到矚目。

Craftsmen's techniques and beauty of patterns packed together.
Ise templates representing warmness of people's hands.
A wide variety of tools are used to produce Some-Komon, of which Ise template, also a traditional art as well, is closely linked with Some-Komon.
Ise templates, primarily produced in Shiroko of Suzuka City, Mie Prefecture, are made with layered Mino paper with sour persimmon pasted in between, and completed by craftsmen who work out the sophisticated patterns by using carving knives designed specially for it. Ise templates are used not only for Edo Komon but also for dyeing process of Kata Yuzen and Yukata, and the patterns are as sophisticated as called "micro space". There are techniques called "Tsukibori", "Kiribori, Dogubori", "Shimabori", and 5 corresponding ones such as "Itoire" to reinforce templates for "Shimabori" and some others. All the techniques are to realize sophistication and warmness of people's hands that machines can't do. In recent years, the templates draw people's attention more and more not only as dyeing tools, but also interior equipment such as for Fusuma, Ramma, Yukimi Shoji, Byobu, and art crafts.

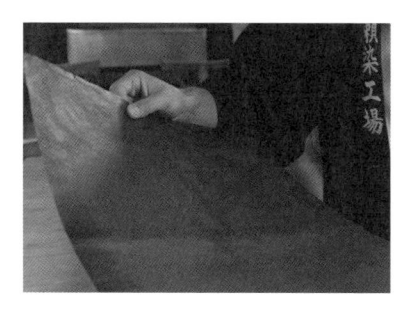

精緻な美が凝縮された伊勢型紙には、職人による技の妙が息づいています。特に細密な柄には彫師の力量が現れます

Ise template, in that sophisticated beauty of patterns are packed together, represents excellence of craftsmen's techniques. Skills of template engravers particularly come into play as delicate as the patterns are.

伊勢模紙凝縮了精緻之美，工匠的巧妙技法使其生動活躍。尤其纖細的圖案更可以呈現出雕模師的功力。

生地の上に型紙を置き、防染糊をヘラで伸ばします。文様によってヘラも変わります。染小紋には欠かせない道具です

Placing a template on a white cloth, put resist paste evenly by a paddle. Different paddle comes on different patterns. An indispensable tool to produce Some-Komon.

將模紙置於布料上，接著用刮刀抹上防染糊。依不同圖案選用不同的刮刀。刮刀是染小紋不可或缺的道具。

伝統工芸士、岩下江美佳さんの型紙と使い込まれたヘラ。彫師と染付職人の技術が揃ってはじめて美しい小紋柄が生まれます

Template, and well-used paddle, that Emika Iwashita, a Traditional Craftsman, uses. Beautiful Komon patterns become real only when techniques of template engraver and dyeing craftsman come together.

傳統工藝士，岩下江美佳小姐的模紙與常用的刮刀。雕模師與染色工匠的技術必須緊密搭配才可創出精美的小紋圖案。

染付職人の仕事を支える張板と、染め上がりを左右する色糊

江戸小紋で用いる、約7メートルの張板(はりいた)は、モミの一枚板です。これを馬と呼ばれるT字型の台に置き、その上に白生地を張って作業が行われます。張板の表面には、粘りけのある「もち粉」が塗られています。生地を張る前に霧吹きをし、ハケでならしたり、塗れぞうきんで拭いたりして、しわが寄らないようにまっすぐに張りつけます。生地をしっかりと固定しないと、染めの段階で柄が曲がってしまうので、これは大切な作業です。そして、前述の型紙を保護するため生地の端にテープを張り、次の工程へ。なお染め付け職人はこの板を7～8枚持っているそうです。

色糊は、染め上がりを左右する大切なもの。糯米(もちごめ)の粉約3割と、米ぬか約7割の割合でつくられます。塩を加えた熱湯を注ぎながら形を整え、蒸籠(せいろう)で蒸した後、練って適度な固さに仕上げます。これが地色を染める糊になります。思い通りの色が上がるよう、一つの色をつくるのにも何種類もの染料を混ぜ、幾度も試験染めをしながら慎重につくられます。温度や湿度によって

輔助染色作業的張板和左右染色效果的色糊

江戶小紋使用的張板約7公尺，是一塊檜木板。將張板放在被稱為馬的T字型台上，接著在板上舖上白底進行作業。在舖上白底前會先噴濕、用刷子掃平，然後用抹布擦拭，最後為避免生皺摺而平舖上白底。假如不確實固定白底的話，會導致在染色階段時圖案出現扭曲，因此這項作業非常重要。接著，為了保護之前提過的模紙，會在白底的邊線貼上膠帶，之後進行下一步。據說染色工匠擁有7～8塊這樣的板子。

色糊是會左右染色效果的要因，以3成糯米粉和7成米糠製作而成。在澆注熱開水時，一邊調整形狀，接著用蒸籠蒸過後，攪拌至一定的硬度後即完成。這就是染色糊的底色。為了調出理想的顏色，即使只是製作一種顏色，也會混合好幾種的染料反覆慎重試染。依溫度和濕度的不同，顏色也會有些許差異，所以染色工匠會自己做筆記留下紀錄並且善加保管。

Hariita, the board which supports the job of dyeing craftsman, and color starch that affects quality of dye finish.

A Hariita, in length of approx. 7 meters used to produce Edo Komon is a solid timber made of fir tree. Placing it on racks in T-shape called Uma, then cover it with a white cloth, Edo Komon is worked out. Top surface of Hariita is coated with sticky rice cake powder. The white cloth is sprayed with water, smooth out with a paddle, and wiped with a damp swabbing cloth to make it placed straightly with no wrinkles. Putting the white cloth firmly in place is an important process to respect, otherwise patterns get out of position when dyeing performed later. Putting adhesive tapes on the edges of white cloth to keep the mentioned template in position, and move onto the next process. Dyeing craftsmen typically have 7 to 8 boards like this.

Color starch is an important element which affects quality of dye finish. It is made from rice cake powder and rice bran, in a ratio of approximately 3:7. After shaping it while pouring boiling water with salt, and steaming it in a steaming basket (Seiroh), the color starch is kneaded for adequate solidity. This becomes starch that marks base color. The starch is carefully made by mixing up different dyes to obtain single color desired and repeat test of dyeing time and time. As the color shows subtly different faces upon temperature and humidity variations, every dyeing craftsman records such data in notebook and stores by its own.

Itaba, where Hariita boards made with fir tree are hung from ceiling. Not many factories are still prepared to supply this type of boards these days. These boards are heritages from older generations.

「板場」的天花板上吊掛著樅木板。聽說現在已很難找到這種板子，那是祖先留下的珍貴遺產。

モミの木の張板が天井に吊られた「板場」。今ではこの板を扱っている所は少ないそう。先代からの遺産です

て色の出方は微妙に変わってしまうので、染付職人はそれぞれ独自でノートにデータを取り保管しています。

張板に生地を張り、染料を均等に塗る「シゴキ」。立描（たてがき）ヘラと呼ばれるヘラを用います

Shigoki process, putting a white cloth on Hariita and placing dye evenly. A paddle called Tategaki is used.

將布料平舖於張板上，均等塗抹染料的「染底色」作業。使用名為立描的刮刀。

Producing base color by mixing base starch and dye. By mixing different dyes and repeat steaming test until desired color is obtained.

將染料與地糊混合調出底色。在此階段，混合染料後須不斷重覆試蒸以調出想要的顏色。

地糊に染料を混ぜ合わせて地色をつくります。
ここで、染料を混ぜ合わせ、出したい色が出るまで試験蒸しを繰り返します

53

手に馴染み、職人と一心同体に。
ヒノキ材のヘラを用いて染め上げる

左にずらりと並んだのは、小紋用の道具の一部です。左の大きなヘラは、立描（たてがき）ヘラ。シゴキヘラとも呼ばれ、色糊を全体に平均に塗り付けるときに使うヘラです。その隣にあるヒノキでできた大駒（おおこま）ヘラです。染付職人は何種類もあるヘラの中で主にこのヘラを使って糊を塗ります。一番右のものは使い込まれてすり減ってしまっています。小宮康孝氏は、小学六年生の夏休みからこのヘラを握り、その持ち方ひとつで父に厳しく鍛えられたといいます。

上に移り、左は細かい文様など糊を均等に置くときに使われる出刃ヘラ。ヘラは文様によって使い分けられますが、手に馴染んだひとつのヘラを使い続ける染付職人もいます。そしてそのお隣は、ボカシ用のハケ大小。繊細な鹿の毛で編まれており、小花模様などを色ボカシするときに使われます。

そして、生地を伸ばすとき使われる地張木（じばりぎ）と呼ばれる木材。空気が入らないよう生地の表面をこすり、布を平らにしっ

用檜木製刮刀進行染色，技藝熟練到與工匠一心同體。左圖中陳列的是製作小紋時用的部分道具。左側較大的刮刀稱為「立描」，又稱為「扱刀」，是將染液平均塗抹至全體所用的刮刀。而位在其旁邊的則是以檜木製成的「大駒刀」，是染色工匠的眾多刮刀中最常被用來塗抹染液的，而最右邊的則可見其長期使用後磨損的模樣。染色專家小宮康孝先生於小學六年級的暑假開始學習正確的刮刀握法，據說，當時他父親小宮康助先生就是用這把刮刀嚴格訓練他的。往上移動，左側是用於使染液能均等分散在織細圖案上的「出刃刀」。依圖案花紋會分別使用不同的刮刀，但也有工匠只用一支自己順手的刮刀。然後，其旁是渲染用的大小毛刷，用纖細的鹿毛編製而成，專用於小花圖案的渲染。接著是稱為「地張木」的木材，主要的用於讓底布能完全伸展開來。為了不讓底布表面殘留氣泡，而使用「地張木」來推，能讓底布完全伸展。這些道具工匠得以完成手工作業，愈用愈順手，最後和工匠們一心同體。這些道具也似乎刻劃著傳統工藝的深奧與工匠們的榮耀。

Fitting comfortably in hand of craftsman, being inseparable as one.
Dye finish by using a paddle made with fir tree.

Those shown in the photo in left are some of tools used to produce Komon. The largest one, far left, is a Tategaki paddle. Also called Shigoki paddle, it is used to put color starch evenly and entirely. The next ones are Okoma paddles made with fir tree. Dyeing craftsmen typically choose this from many others when putting starch. The one far right is worn down because of being used throughout years. It is said that dyeing expert Yasutaka Komiya, whose father is Kosuke Komiya, started to learn how to use this paddle since summer vacation when he was 6th grade of elementary school, and used to be put through the mill by his father even on how to hold it in hand.Moving up, the one shown far left is a Deba paddle used to put starch evenly for delicate patterns. Generally, paddle to use is selected from pattern to pattern, but some craftsmen keep using only one type whichi he/she feels fit comfortably into the hand. The next ones are small and large paddles for feathering. Woven with fine deer pelage, these are used to perform feathering on patterns such as small flowers.The next one is a piece of wood called Jibarigi, used to stretch white cloth. Having slided on the surface of white cloth not to allow air to come underneath, it is used to keep the cloth straight and placed firmly.Tools, that support craftsmen's handwork. Well used throughout years, and becoming inseparable with each of craftsmen, the tools start asserting the depth of aesthetics of traditional arts and pride of the craftsmen.

下段はヘラ各種。上段は、ボカシ用のハケ。
江戸小紋では、大駒(おおこま)ヘラと、立描(たてがき)ヘラ、しごきヘラなどを使います。

A variety of paddles, in bottom raw. The one in upper raw is a brush for feathering.
Okoma, Tategaki, Shigoki, and some other paddles are used for Edo Komon

下方為各式刮刀。上方為調色用的毛刷。江戸小紋的製作使用大駒刮刀、立描刮刀與染底色刮刀等進行作業。

鹿毛を束ねた丸ハケは、小花模様の濃淡をつける色ボカシなどに多く使用されます

A brush tipped with woven deer pelage, regularly used to perform feathering of colors to adjust contrast of patterns such as small flower.

圓刷以鹿毛製成,多用於小圖案的上色與其濃淡的調整。

地張木(じばりぎ)で生地を押さえることで、張板にしっかりと張りつけます

Pressing down by Jibarigi, white cloth becomes firmly placed on Hariita.

用地張木押好底布,使其能紮實伸展在張板上。

かりと張りつけます。
職人の手仕事を支える道具。使い込まれ、職人と一心同体となった道具には伝統工芸の奥深さと、職人の誇りが刻まれているようです。

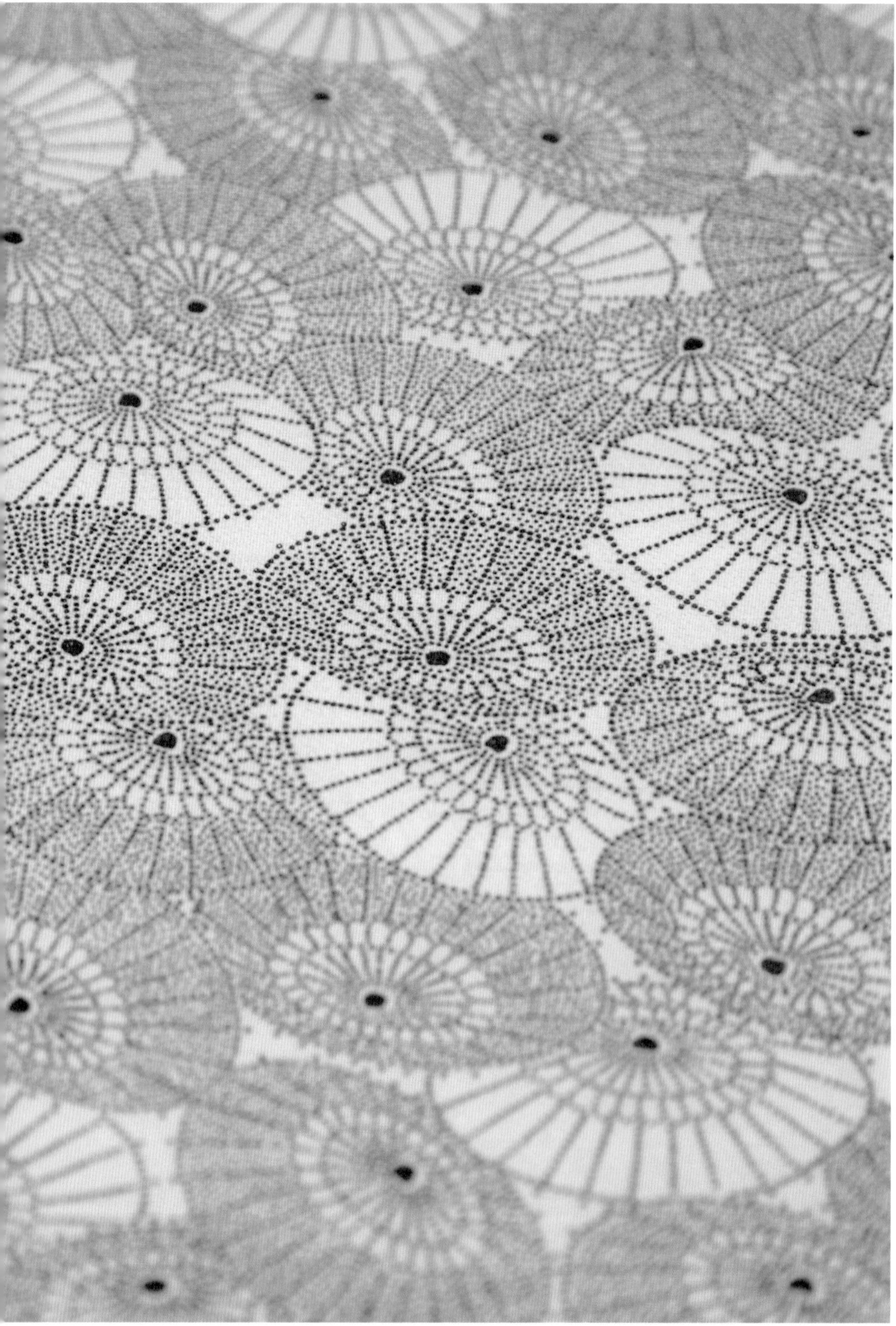

岩下江美佳・作品
Works of Emika Iwashita
岩下江美佳小姐的作品

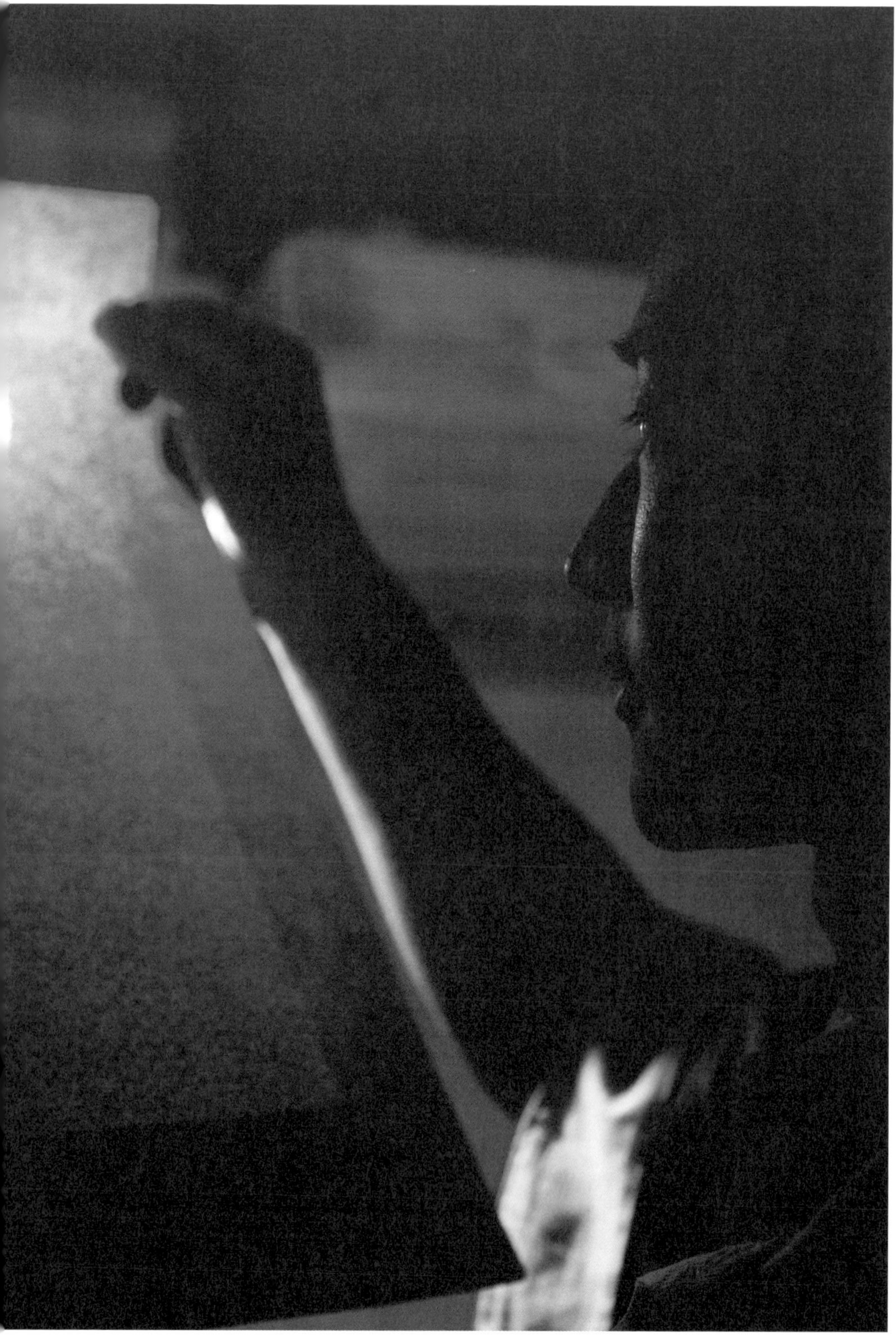

江戸小紋の文様

Patterns of Edo Komon

江戶小紋的圖案

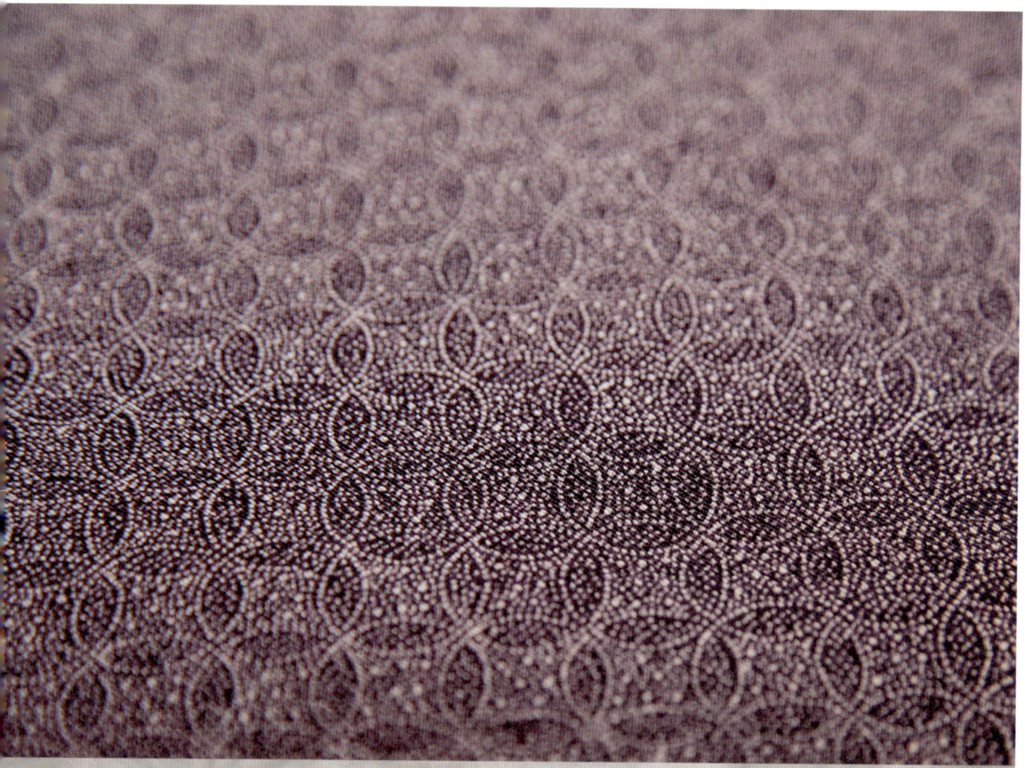

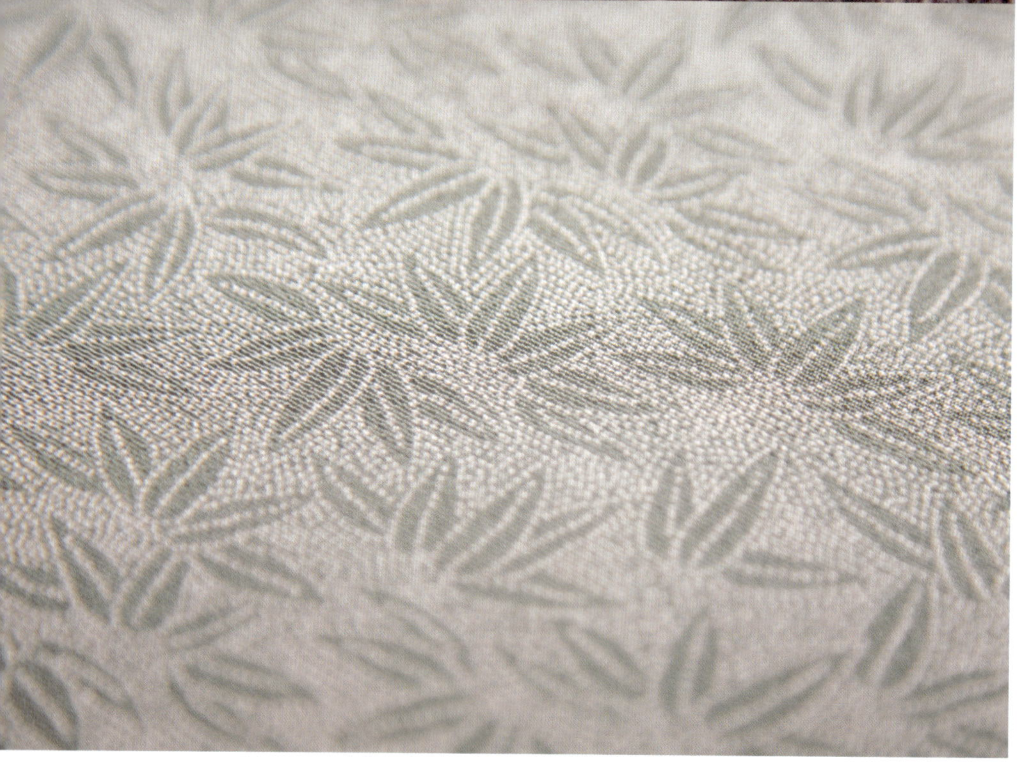

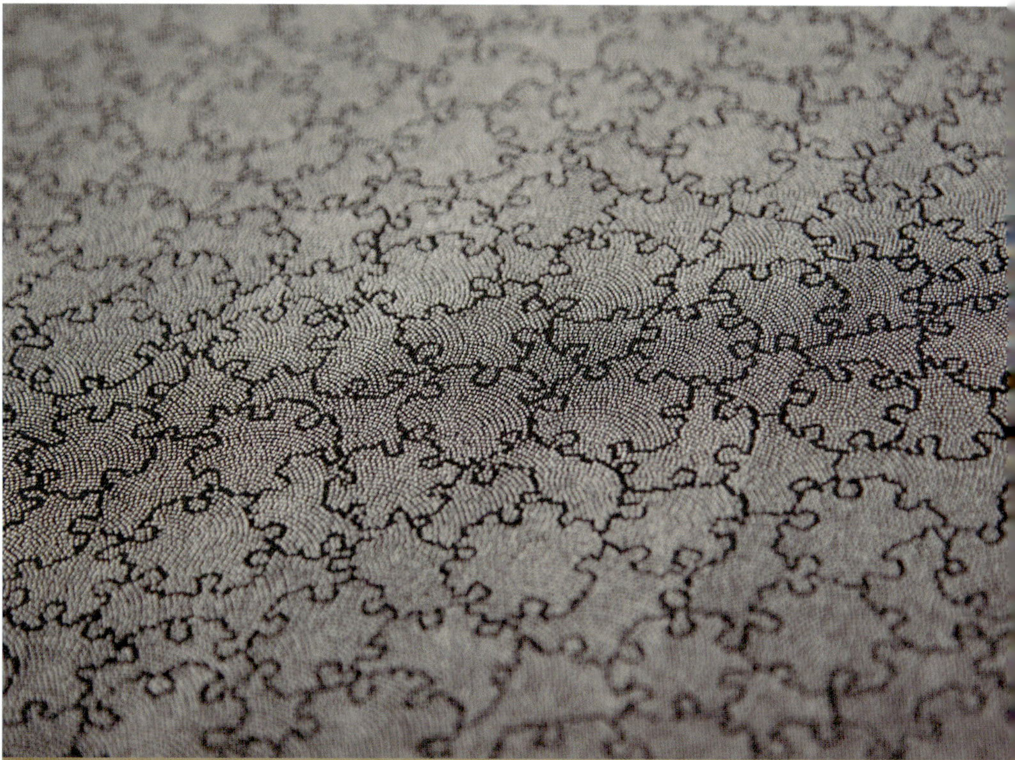

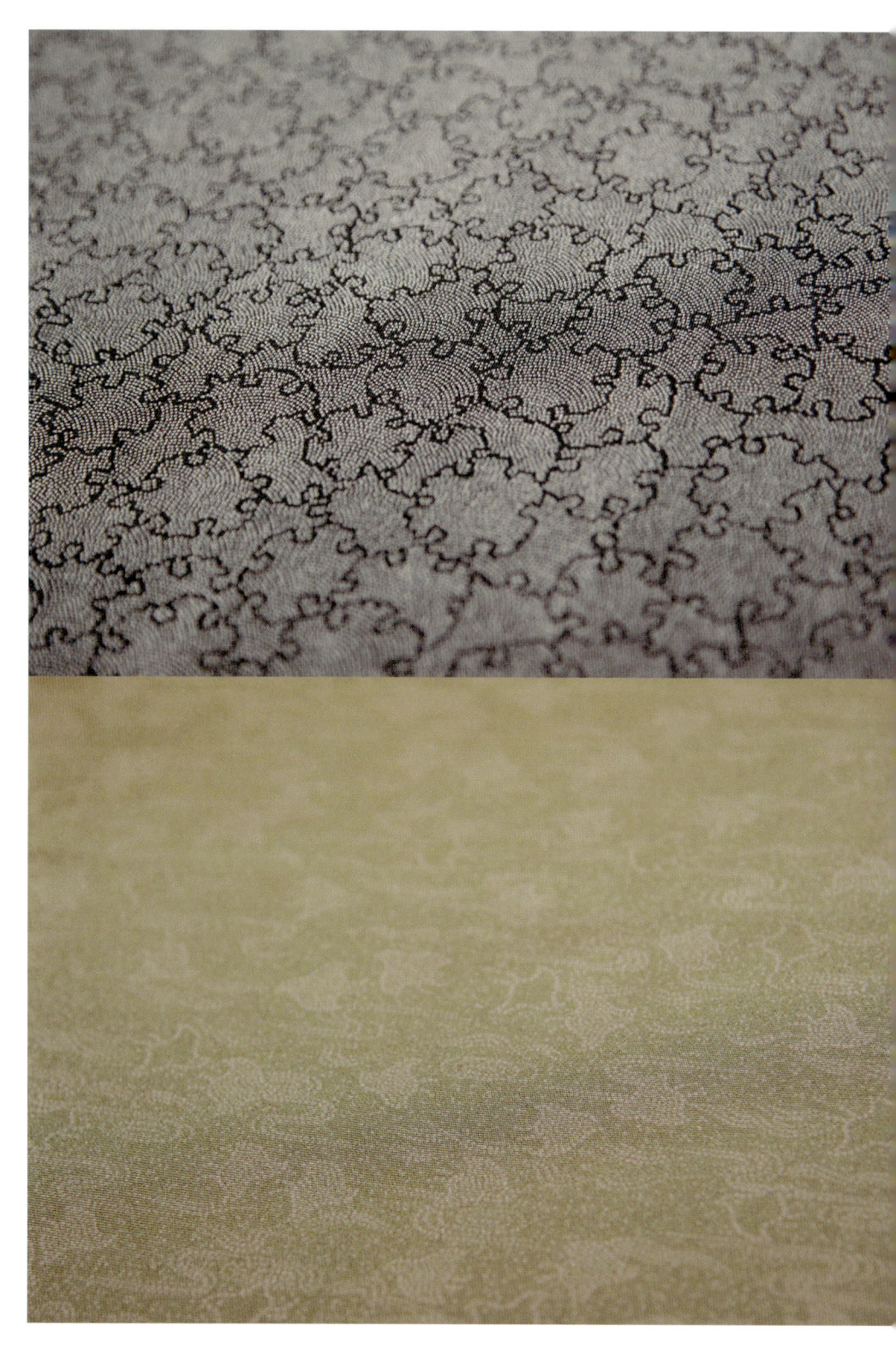

細かな模様と単色が融合。
隠れたお洒落で人々を魅了

一般的に小紋とは、型紙を用いて小さい模様を彩った着物を指します。中でも江戸小紋（東京染小紋）は、微細な幾何学模様と単彩が特徴です。単色ながらも、粋で格調高い雰囲気を備えています。また、模様が細かいので、遠くからだと無地に見えますが、近づくにつれて現れてくる美しい模様に思わずうっとり。この隠れたお洒落は、江戸の粋を感じさせます。着物のほか、マフラーやランプシェードなど、今の時代の要素を取り入れた江戸小紋も生産されています。

融合纖細圖案與單一色彩。
令人讚嘆不已的隱藏式時尚。
一般來說，所謂的小紋是指利用模紙製作，搭配小巧圖案的和服。其中，江戶小紋(東京染小紋)以細微的幾何圖案與單一色彩為特徵。雖為單色，但仍蘊涵著經典氣質與高雅格調。另外，因為圖案纖細，遠看像是素色，但近觀就會被其呈現出的美感所吸引。這種難以發現的隱藏式時尚，讓人感覺到這就是江戶的氣質。除了和服以外，圍巾和燈罩等也製作出一些融入現代化要素的江戶小紋。

Delicate patterns and single color come together.
Less self-assertive dandyism makes people enchanted.
In general, Komon stands for Kimono with small patterns realized by using templates. Edo Komon (Tokyo Some-Komon) in particular is featured with fine geometric patterns and single color. Even with a single color, Edo Komon is in its style and spirited with elegance. Also, as the patterns are small, it looks as if no patterns when looking from a distance, but as coming closer you will find the beautiful patterns and be fascinated with it. This way of less self-assertive dandyism represents the style of Edo. Not only for Kimono, Edo Komon is now deployed to some others such as scarfs and lampshades, adopting trends today.

すべて「廣瀬染工場」作品

All are works by Hirose Senkojo

全部皆為的「廣瀬染工坊」的作品

極雪輪（ごくゆきわ）／ Gokuyukiwa 極雪輪

七宝／ Shippo 七寶

千鳥／ Chidori 千鳥

笹／ Sasa 笹竹

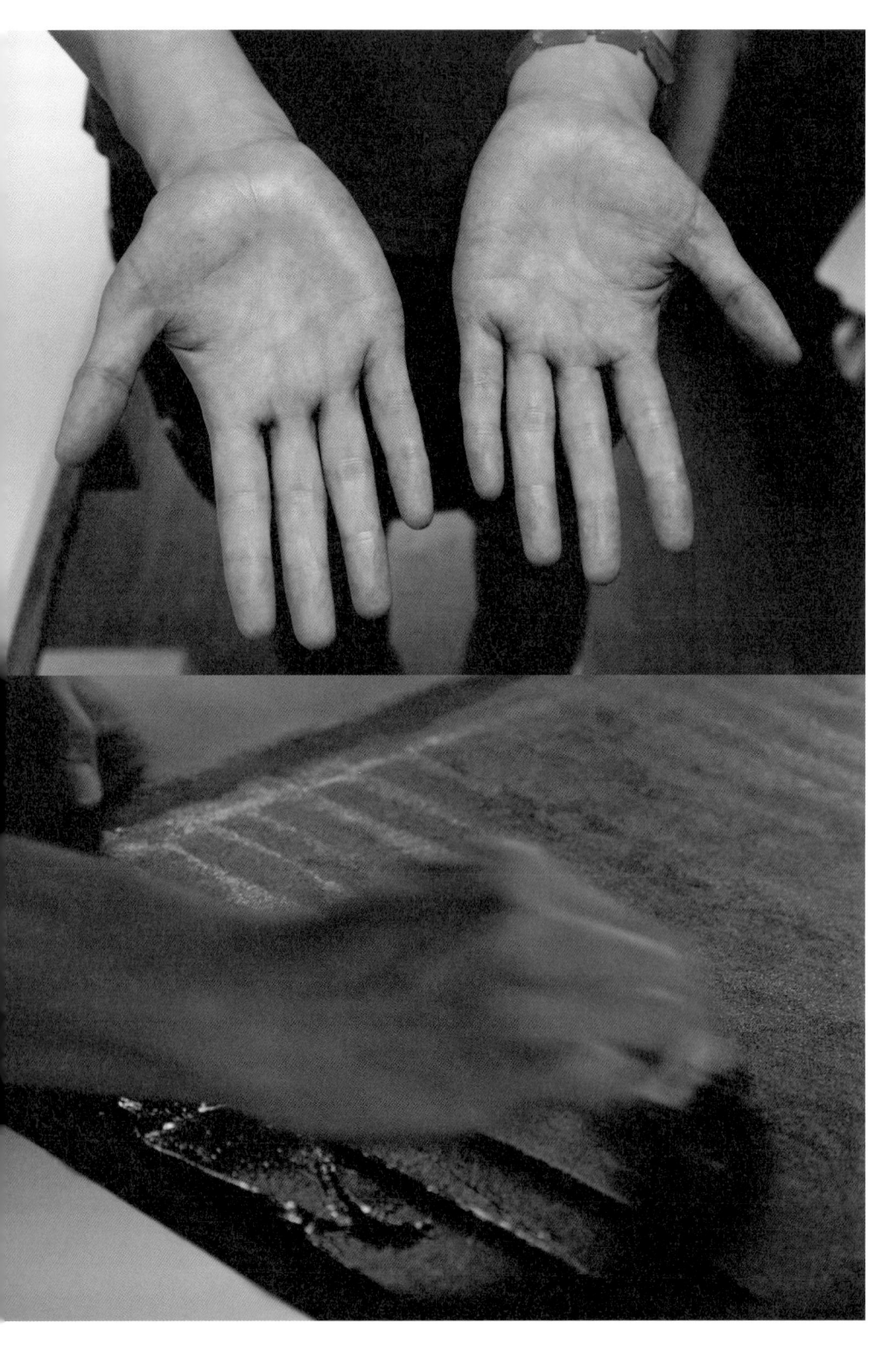

染付職人への道

Paths to Become a Dyeing Craftsman

成為染色工匠的路程

写実的、絵画的など、多くの意匠を凝らして染め上げる

絹、綿、麻などの繊維製品を、手描き染め、型染め、絞り染めといったさまざまな技法で染め上げる職人です。力強い単色、写実的な草花模様、幾何学模様と技法や産地によって意匠はさまざまです。中でも有名なのが友禅染（ゆうぜんぞめ）。扇絵師で活躍していた宮崎友禅斎が、京都で染技法を確立したのをきっかけに、京友禅、加賀友禅、江戸友禅へと広がっていったのです。また、染めの工程には、デザインの立案から仕上げまで行う一貫体制と完全分業体制があります。どちらも奥深い着物の美しさを創出し、伝統技法を受け継ぎながら発展を続けています。

True-to-nature and painterly, making the best use of multi techniques for dyeing.
Craftsmen, who perform dyeing on a variety of textiles such as silk, cotton, and linen, adopting a variety of techniques including Tegaki-zome, Kata-zome, and Shibori-zome. The design may be in bold single color, true-to-nature patterns of vegetation, or geometric patterns, varies upon techniques used and the place of production. One of well-known is Yuzen-zome. Originated by Yuzenzai Miyazaki, who used to play an active role as a fan painter and established a dyeing method in Kyoto, it became spread to Kyo Yuzen, Kaga Yuzen, and Edo Yuzen. There are two different ways of dyeing process; one is consecutive that all from design making to finalizing product are done in one series, and the other is division of labor. Both of them are proven ways to realize depth of beauty of Kimono and continuing to develop while upholding the traditional techniques.

凝聚寫實性、繪畫性等多項創意所製作而成
將蠶絲、綿布、麻布等纖維製品用手繪染、染布印模、夾染等技術製作染布的工匠。力道強勁的單一色彩、寫實性的花草圖案、幾何圖案，以及因技巧與產地不同而產生的創意也各有千秋。在這之中最有名的算是友禪染。宮崎友禪齋是位非常傑出的扇繪師，當時他在京都以確立染布技術為契機，使其影響力擴及京友禪、加賀友禪、江戶友禪。另外，在染布作業中，從設計定案到完成製作，分為一貫體制與完全分業體制。不管哪種都能創作出和服的深奧之美，因而得以傳承傳統技法並持續發展。

自分の色を創りだす。分業制は職人同士が刺激

一貫体制の場合は、立案から実施するため、着物に自分のデザインを確立したい人におすすめです。分業体制は、指示通りの色になっているかを判断する能力が必要ですが、染色作家や加飾の職人など、さまざまなプロと切磋琢磨し合えるのが魅力のひとつです。染色で大切なのは、「主人公＝着る人」という心。染付職人は、あくまでも脇役。着る人が、より美しく、より洗練されて見えるように染め上げるのが職人です。一方、友禅染のように画期的なデザインを開発すれば、技法に自分の名前を付けられる夢もあります。

Creating your own color. Craftsmen can learn from each other under division of labor way.
Under consecutive way, your work starts from initial conception, therefore this way of work may fit those who want to reflect the original design in Kimono. As for the way of division of labor, you will be required to be enough skilled to evaluate if the color appeared is as specified, but one of the attractive points is that you can enjoy learning from each other, from professionals such as dyeing artists and decorating craftsmen. The most important thing for you to keep in mind is "Principal is the people who puts on it". Dyeing craftsmen are supporting players in any case. The work craftsmen must do is to finish dyeing in order to make the customer putting the Kimono look beutiful and sophisticated. On the other hand, you can expect to follow a dream to put your own name on your work, once you create an innovative design like Yuzen-zome.

創作出屬於自己的色彩。分業制能工匠們有所激發
一貫體制是指從定案到執行，所以推薦給想要創作自我設計風格和服的人。分業體制是雖然必須有判斷是否要照指示製作的能力，但對染色作家或裝飾工匠來說，能與眾多專家切磋琢磨是其魅力之一。染色最重要的是「主角＝穿著的人」的心。染色工匠只是個配角。工匠的執著可以讓穿著的人看起來更美、更高雅。另一方面，如果能開發出像友禪染這樣劃時代的設計風格，也可以夢想像友禪一樣以自己的名字為技法命名。

岩下江美佳・作品
Works of Emika Iwashita
岩下江美佳小姐的作品

染色専門の学校で学ぶ。
職人の多くは関西、北陸、関東に

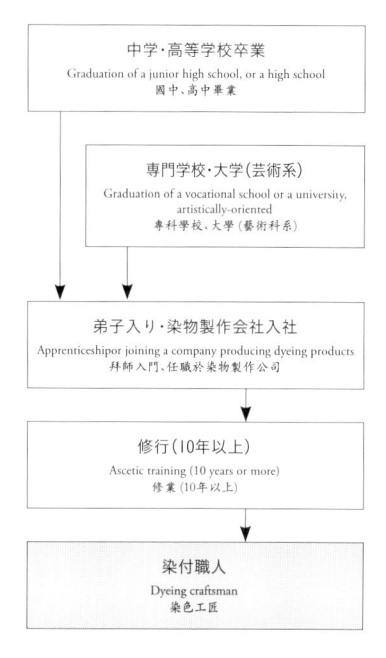

着物染色工芸科を擁する学校を始め、美術系の大学や専門学校などで学ぶことができます。多くの場合で職場となる染物製造会社は、友禅染を代表に関西から北陸、関東などに分布。熟練したワザ、精神力、デザイン感覚を習得するのに、10年以上の修業期間が必要だといわれています。

```
┌─────────────────────────────┐
│ 中学・高等学校卒業              │
│ Graduation of a junior high │
│ school, or a high school    │
│ 國中、高中畢業                  │
└──────────────┬──────────────┘
               │
               ▼
┌─────────────────────────────┐
│ 専門学校・大学(芸術系)          │
│ Graduation of a vocational  │
│ school or a university,     │
│ artistically-oriented       │
│ 專科學校、大學(藝術科系)        │
└──────────────┬──────────────┘
               │
               ▼
┌─────────────────────────────┐
│ 弟子入り・染物製作会社入社       │
│ Apprenticeshipor joining a  │
│ company producing dyeing    │
│ products                    │
│ 拜師入門、任職於染物製作公司     │
└──────────────┬──────────────┘
               │
               ▼
┌─────────────────────────────┐
│ 修行(10年以上)                 │
│ Ascetic training            │
│ (10 years or more)          │
│ 修業(10年以上)                 │
└──────────────┬──────────────┘
               │
               ▼
┌─────────────────────────────┐
│ 染付職人                      │
│ Dyeing craftsman            │
│ 染色工匠                      │
└─────────────────────────────┘
```

Learning at schools dedicated in dyeing.
Large proportions of craftsmen are distributed in Kansai, Hokuriku, and Kanto.
You can learn dyeing at schools such as those offering course of Kimono dyeing craftwork, art colleges, and vocational schools. Large propotions of companies producing dyeing products, represented by Yuzen-zome for example, are distributed in Kansai, Hokuriku, and Kanto. It is said that apprenticeship for more than 10 years is required to master skilled techniques, achieve mental strength, and design sense.

在染布的專業學校學習。
許多工匠都在關西、北陸、關東。
可以學習的地點包括設有和服染工藝科系的學校、美術系列的大學或專科學校等。多數情況下，未來的就業方向多為染物製造公司，以友禪為代表，分布於關西到北陸、關東等。一般認為，光是學習磨練技巧、精神力、設計感，這些就必須花費10年以上的修業時間。

職人という生き方
江戸小紋

本書編集スタッフ

構成　　　　　　木下のぞみ
取材・文　　　　ニッポンのワザドットコム編集部
デザイン・装丁　棟田夏子
写真　　　　　　富野博則
校正　　　　　　荒木さおり（ブレインカフェ）
英訳　　　　　　古賀知憲

職人という生き方 江戸小紋

二〇一一年十月　第一刷発行	
編者	ニッポンのワザドットコム編集部
	Ⓒ有限会社ブレインカフェ
発行者	木下のぞみ
発行所	有限会社ブレインカフェ
	東京都中央区銀座四丁目十一―六
	島倉ビル三階
	電話　〇三―五一四八―五八一八（代表）
	http://www.braincafe.net
印刷・製本	シナノ書籍印刷株式会社

定価はカバーに表示してあります。
造本には充分注意しておりますが、万一乱丁・落丁がございましたらお取り替えいたします。
本書の無断複写（コピー）は著作権法上の例外を除き、著作権の侵害になります。

Printed in Japan　ISBN 978-4-905416-01-2　C0072